Dare to Change Life series

A Shift
toward
Purpose

Secrets to an
Amazing Career

By
Millen Livis, M.S., M.B.A.

Legal Disclosure
All information contained in this book is intended to be a sharing of knowledge from the research and experience of the author. It came from sources believed to be accurate, but no profit or earnings guarantees, expressed or implied, can be made.

The information contained herein is meant to be used to educate the reader and is in no way intended to provide customized career counseling. Personal career counseling may be obtained from a qualified career counselor.

Dedication

To you, a brave soul, who chose or is about to choose to follow your true self in spite of fear, and step out of the comfort zone in pursuit of a meaningful career and purposeful life.

Contents

Contents

Free Bonus
"A Shift toward Purpose" Audiobook

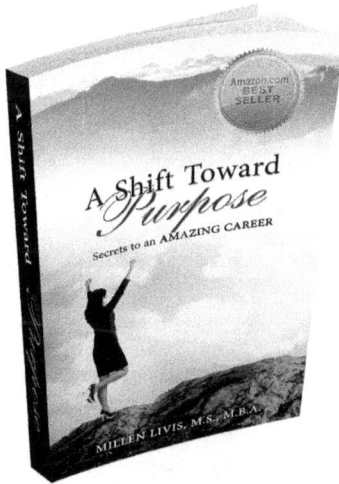

If you'd like to listen to the audiobook version of "A Shift toward Purpose: Secrets to an Amazing Career" while you follow along with the book or walk or... drive, you can download it for free for a limited time at **millenlivis.com/purpose**

Dare
to Change
Life

Introduction

If you are unhappy with your work right now, whether you are in your twenties or your fifties, stop blaming yourself for making the wrong choices that led you here. You made the best choices you had at the time considering the awareness, knowledge and understanding you had before.

You cannot change your past but you can change the direction of your life now if you choose to trust your 'gut.' You are well equipped with your mind and your soul – your intuition, your talents, and your aspirations – to have a meaningful, successful and authentic life.

The mind's perspective is practical, rational and grounded, which is very important as long as it doesn't limit or paralyze you with fear and indecision. The soul's perspective is expansive, exciting and positive. However, choosing only the soul's perspective may leave you ungrounded and disillusioned at best.

In my opinion, the solution to a happy and successful life is balance. Try not to spend too much time focusing only on your rational mind but also do not get carried away just by your soul's desires. Strive for balance. Neale Donald Walsch wrote in one of his inspirational emails that "The mind and the soul must work together if you are to experience true bliss."

If you want to have a meaningful and gratifying career, if you want to find your heartfelt purpose in life and experience peace, you must be aware of the duality of your existence (physical and spiritual) and nourish and strengthen both – your mind and your soul.

It is my intention in this book to inspire your beautiful and genuine self to trust yourself and your intuition, to recover your self-confidence and self-reliance. I want you to love yourself enough to work through your fear of change and the unknown, to clear and release your emotional blockages and activate your creative potential.

I would be delighted if the messages in this book resonate with you. I would love to be able to assist you in making a shift toward a life blessed with meaning, faith, purpose and contentment. It is my joy and honor to offer guidance to women seeking authentic self-expression and ways to be their best and serve the world best. I admire you and am proud of you for having the courage to choose yourself and follow your gut.

CHAPTER 1

Why Do You Behave the Way You Do?

"What lies before us, what lies behind us, is nothing compared to what lies within us."

~ Ralph Waldo Emerson

Many times I have been asked, "Why do you need to write books? Why do you constantly search for ways to serve, to share, to express yourself? You are a human *being* not a human *doing*! Can't you just *be*?"

I've heard these questions from my husband and others often enough to start asking myself, "Why do humans behave the way we do? What drives us?"

Whatever experience you're going through now – health challenges, a relationship break up, betrayal, loss of job, financial losses, personal rejection or a career change – your perception of the challenges and reactions to 'problems' in life conceal deep hidden needs for something more fundamental than may appear on a surface.

Hierarchy of Human Needs

We rarely (or never) make the effort to dig deeper into our feelings in order to discover the underlying reasons for our frustrations, desires, motivations or pain.

In the meantime, at the root of what we perceive as problems in life lay many unsatisfied *human needs: to belong, to be loved, to feel safe, to be acknowledged, to feel significant.* A psychologist by the name of Abraham Maslow first introduced the hierarchy of human needs back in the 1960s. There were five categories in Maslow's original list of human needs:

- **Biological/Psychological**
- **Safety**
- **Love**
- **Esteem**
- **Self-Actualization**

Although there have been a few modifications to Maslow's hierarchy of human needs, I would like to offer you my own summarized interpretation of the *human needs hierarchy* in the following order of importance:

1. **Need for physical comfort.** Having air, food, water and shelter; having enough sleep, not experiencing physical pain.
2. **Need to feel safe.** This translates into having enough material possessions and a reliable source of money/

income to have perceived security now and in the future.

3. **Need for connection.** We have an inherent need to belong, to have companionship, to be accepted, to feel connected with an individual or be part of a group.

4. **Need to feel significant, acknowledged, valued, recognized, seen and heard.**

5. **Need to be self-actualized.** To develop and express our talents and expertise to benefit the world, to function at our highest potential.

6. **Need to contribute.** To give, to help, to serve in some way.

Regardless of your background, age, race, religion or line of work, you are driven by these fundamental human needs. This universal force is a dominant drive behind your feelings, motivations and actions.

What About J.O.B.?

I have heard a few versions for the acronym J.O.B., from Just Over Broke to Just Obey Boss to Join Our Bureaucracy. The superior and arrogant attitude about having a job in our modern society is disturbing.

You are naturally programmed to satisfy your inherent needs. While you were very young, you expected your parents to take care of you – provide food, shelter, medical care, express love and affection. However, later in life, you go through a 'separation phase' when your expectations for satisfying your primal needs begin to shift to yourself, to being self-reliant.

Teenagers and young adults, who have part-time jobs while attending school, learn earlier in life how to earn, spend and save money. They usually grow up more mature and better adept at taking care of themselves and respect any kind of work as a result of their appreciation for the ability to be autonomous.

Work that allows you to take care of yourself and your family must be appreciated and respected, even if it's not what you would like to do in your life. In my opinion, it is preposterous to speak without respect about any *job* and refuse work because it's below you while expecting others (family, government, society) to provide for your basic needs.

It is essential from a physical and spiritual perspective to feel that you can with-stand challenges in life and be self-reliant. It builds character and endurance. Always find appreciation for the work you have at the moment and view it as a stepping stone to your ultimate *'dream work.'*

I recall in my early thirties working in a flower shop, getting paid a minimum wage and thinking that I could do 'bigger and better things' as a trained physicist and an experienced software engineer. But various circumstances in my life at that time did not allow me to do 'bigger and better.'

I realized how fortunate I was to have a job that was providing for my family's basic needs. My attitude shifted, I became more grateful and positive and soon moved on to a more satisfying job, which became yet another stepping stone for my ultimate 'dream work.'

Having a vision of your 'dream work' is as important as seeing value in your current work and feeling appreciation for the benefits it offers. Keeping your dream alive programs your subconscious to navigate through life in a way that allows you to collect the necessary skills and experiences to get you to the work you feel you were meant to do, your 'dream work.'

Awareness Helps

Since human beings exist on both the physical and spiritual plane, some needs are more pertinent to the physical realm and others to the spiritual one. The first three items in the human needs hierarchy are primal human needs that, when satisfied, help you function with comfort in the physical realm. Once these basic needs have been met, you can then focus on the last three needs, which pertain to the spiritual category or your *true self*.

Being aware of the needs hierarchy doesn't make you 'needy' (unless you *act needy*)! You will be more compassionate if you remain aware of the fact that every moment you are—and everyone around you is—trying to satisfy individual physical, psychological and spiritual needs.

The importance of each need category differs for different people and conflicting needs may cause intra- and interpersonal problems. For instance, you are not crazy if:

- your well-paid job didn't make you feel significant and valued and you decided to resign and do something else
- your successful business doesn't bring you a sense of

meaning and purpose and you want to stop and start something else

• your need for self-actualization may not be welcomed or understood by a friend or a partner

Awareness, patience and understanding of the natural progression of your needs over time, as well as respect for other people's needs, will help you to be more tolerant and have a healthy attitude and balanced state of mind.

You create your life by choosing your attitude, developing a personal philosophy and deciding on your actions. Jim Rohn wrote, "Activity, attitude and philosophy create results."

If you are not pleased with the results in your life, the most important and effective levers you have at your disposal to change the results are those three – your attitude, your personal philosophy and your actions.

CHAPTER 2

How Do You Know it's Time to Change?

"There are times when we may fool ourselves. There are times when we can fool others. But we can never fool our body. It is the most sensitive barometer of our inner world."

– Sherrill Sellman

I felt stuck, functioning on autopilot. Although my job provided a comfortable living, it was unsatisfying. I suddenly felt that I was wasting my life away, yet still wasn't sure if it would be wise to change the course of my career and risk the financial comfort and certainty that I was longing for. Like most people, I don't like change and am afraid of life's changes....

Nonetheless, I have *predisposition toward taking action in spite of fear.* And I want you to have it too!

Dare to Choose Yourself

A lot of people live as if their life is just a rehearsal, while paralyzed by envy, self-doubts and fears – chronically discontent about their life, with little joy and satisfaction.

Many do not go beyond whining, complaining and resenting. There are endless excuses, blame, justifications for procrastination and yet…lack of action.

The self-doubt, envy and self-pity blocks your ability to see clearly how powerful, capable and special you are. The fog of fear prevents you from seeing that you can break free from this imprisonment. While it's important to manage risk and act responsibly in your professional life, there is a point when you must make a decision – to choose yourself.

Like everybody else, you probably have an army of advisors – parents, friends, family members, coaches and managers. While it's wise to seek support and guidance outside of yourself, you need to discern what resonates with you – your values, your aspirations, your supportive beliefs – and assert your own decisions.

Confident decisiveness is required for having a successful career. You can develop it by *trusting your inner knowing, by practicing self-reliance and by strengthening your resilience.* When you act in spite of your self-doubt and fear, believing in your ability to achieve your goals, no matter what, you reclaim your inner power and exude confident decisiveness.

Listen to Your Intuition

You may work for years at your job or business, feeling bored or fed up, suffering in silence from dissatisfaction and lack of acknowledgement but not realizing that this prolonged internal stress destroys your health and diminishes your self-confidence.

When you experience prolonged stress, whether it's physical, emotional, mental or all of the above, you literally make yourself sick. That's when you must *procrastinate no more because you're overdue for a change!*

As a spiritual being going through a physical experience, you are well-equipped to use your inner navigation system – your intuition, your gut feeling, your insight or *Inner Advisor*. When going through challenging experiences, I remind myself and others of the well-known saying: 'Let Go and Let God.' You are able to transcend the limitations of your mind and access this *Collective Consciousness* or the *Infinite Source of Wholeness*.

Albert Einstein wrote, "The intuitive mind is a sacred gift and the rational mind is a faithful servant. We have created a society that honors the servant and has forgotten the gift."

There are various ways to connect to the Universal Consciousness: prayer (asking), gratitude (expressing), meditation (receiving), or feeling – observing sensations in your body when you ask yourself specific questions. I practice all of the above but find the 'body barometer' to be the most efficient for myself. The body is a unique tool that you can use to connect to your Inner Advisor, to your higher self.

Lee Milteer writes in her book *Feel & Grow Rich*: "If we deny and cut off our intuition, then we get trapped by concepts learned through our programmed minds…. You must have an integration of analytical and intuitive thinking."

I invite you to try an exercise to determine whether it's time to make a change in your professional life. Visualize yourself being at work, doing what you usually do, feeling what you usually feel while at work. Then ask yourself: "Is this current job (or a business) a good fit for my aspirations and talents?" Now observe the sensations in your body.

Do you feel heavy or light, excited and inspired or painfully disturbed? Your body will give you an answer with positive certainty. If you feel tightness in your chest, muscle tension and overall un-ease, then it's time to change course. *Act now.*

CHAPTER 3

It's Time to Change, But to Do What?

"Every adversity, every failure, every heartache carries with it the seed on an equal or greater benefit."

~ Napoleon Hill

Since I was a young girl, I've wanted to live life without regrets. Such resolve forced me to take on more risk than normal and face fear while accepting the consequences of my actions.

This determination led me to quit my comfortable Wall Street career path and become an entrepreneur. Although the consequences of this decision were very challenging financially and emotionally, deep in my gut I knew that I would get sick unless I explored other career options. Choosing the status quo while being unfulfilled and discontent would be a personal failure in my mind because I perceive failure in life as not trying to follow your inner guidance rather than not achieving the desired outcome.

Practice Self-love and Commit to Your Truth

If you experience fear and self-doubt, relax! These emotions naturally arise when you are considering making big changes in life. The key is not to linger in the state of fear and self-doubt, and to re-focus on what's really important to you. Ask yourself the following questions:

- *"Are you willing to feel stuck or trapped until this feeling will make you physically sick?"*

- *"Who do you think you are not?"*

You were born with an abundance of creative energy, with unique gifts and talents. They may or may not be grandiose – being a teacher, a mother or a therapist may not carry societal prestige like other professions (e.g. doctor or lawyer) but *you can only succeed by living life true to yourself. Chasing prestigious or lucrative professions/ jobs that are not right for you is like wearing designer dresses that don't fit. Learn to be comfortable in your own skin, learn to love who you are.*

Self-love, while essential, is a foreign concept for most people. There are many facets to this concept: eating well and resting well, loving more and worrying less, accepting and honoring your uniqueness and peculiarities, believing that you are enough and that you are lovable.

In this book, I want you to focus on your

professional career because self-actualization is another facet of self-love and your professional life affects your health and your happiness.

You must love yourself enough to truly believe that *living at your highest potential* is not a caprice or a whim but a powerful inherent force, a drive that you are born with. It's imperative that you honor this drive if you want to find contentment and tranquility in life. It's a great personal tragedy to die without knowing who you really could have been....

In spite of whatever challenging situations you encounter in your life, *Never Ever Stop Loving and Believing in Yourself.* Let go of self-judgments, unrealistic expectations, attachments, self-pity and envy.

Don't let any crushing circumstances crash you – remember that *you are a spark of the Higher Power and are not alone.* Practice *self-love,* commit to being *true to yourself* in spite of your fears; ask for help if needed.

Like most things in life, finding your career path may take you through many iterations and zigzags. Very few folks have certainty about their life direction at an early age. Most people, including myself, have or will change careers several times in their lives, while constantly evolving, accumulating new knowledge, understanding and awareness.

Gather Your Career Vision

When you experience an impasse in your career (or life in general) it is hard to think things through because your mind is overwhelmed by repetitive thoughts of impasse, anxiety and fear. You often feel depressed and ashamed as a result of being dissatisfied with your job (or business), being unable to focus and feeling stuck.

Herein lies the mystery and paradox of life: somewhere inside you there is a *knowing* of who you really are and what you want. You don't need to 'design' your career vision; instead, you can gather the knowledge and insight that would lead you to an inspiring and satisfying life. Of course, it's easier said than done! Nonetheless, it's not only probable, it's possible. Yes, you can 'mine' your vision!

Your subconscious is filled with a barrage of messages from our society, culture and influential people in your life (parents, teachers, counselors). They suggest which colleges provide the best opportunities, which professions are best to enter, which jobs are prestigious and how to succeed in life. These messages form your image of the 'good life' and at some point may lead to experiencing *disharmony with what you feel and do.*

I believe that the experience of impasse is a wake-up call to alarm you about the accumulated incongruence between what you learned and what you feel. It is an indicator of a need for correction in your perceptions and your personal philosophy, a shift in your awareness.

You must quiet the noise in your head about having a lack of skills or knowledge. Forget about the 'how and when.' Instead, *have faith that you will find the clarity and vision of work and success that feels right for you!*

There is no precise formula or shortcut that I know of to get you over the impasse – you will have to do the work. A new vision of your career (and life) can be gathered through various ways and I will provide a brief overview of some of the ways that I used in my own life and career:

1. **Uncover your life-long passions.**
2. **Observe what kind of work excites you.**
3. **Know your WHY.**
4. **Ask yourself and write your answers to career-specific questions (see below).**
5. **Visualize – Experience Your Desire ('It'); Activate All Your Senses.**
6. **Ask God for guidance.**

Take time to venture into a fascinating journey of self-discovery. If you are like most people, it may take a while for you to find your place in the world, to feel like 'this is it', and to say, "I will overcome any obstacle I may encounter…" whether it's debt, lack of prestige or fear.

Be patient with yourself as you are mining your embedded talents. "Follow your bliss," as Joseph Campbell wrote. This bliss or sense of excitement is a sign of important self-discovery.

1. Uncover Your Lifelong Passions

Most likely, you have favorite activities, books and conversation topics, your desired work environment, people whose work you admire, etc. In other words, gather a combination of your interests that makes your life more enjoyable. Start paying attention to your lifelong interests – they will help reveal your most persistent interests, your passions.

For example, observe what kind of books you have in your home library or which section you gravitate to browse through while in a bookstore or a public library. Notice patterns in your interests and preferences – what topics, activities, places and people carry the most meaning for you.

2. Observe What Kind of Work Excites You

Write a list of different professions and *ask yourself:* "Which one would be right for me?" Observe the sensations in your body. Do you feel enthusiasm, excitement or fear?

When you see or hear about other people being an artist, a doctor, an engineer, a stock market trader, a business manager, a psychologist or a teacher, a coach or a diplomat, do you get the feeling that you would love to do that yourself? Do you feel excited at the prospect of seeing yourself in their shoes?

3. Know Your WHY

Notice where your attention goes when you think about different professions. Are you focused on what people with these professions earn rather than who they become and what they do?

If your primary focus is on the potential reward, although it is very important, you may miss finding out about your own embedded life-long interests. Money, prestige or fame alone will not substitute for the joy of finding satisfying work, the 'bliss' of self-actualizing.

Knowing your WHY, your true reason for wanting a particular professional career, will help you discern whether it is your true life-long passion or just the idea of a lucrative career and prestigious social status that was burned into your subconscious by society, family or friends.

Your WHY must be really important to you, beyond the desires, wishes, opinions and suggestions of others. It should feel right at your core in order to get you through any challenges along the way. Be aware of your WHY....

4. Write Your Answers to Career-specific Questions

Find a way to bring your mind to stillness. You may meditate, go for a walk in nature or relax by the river or an ocean. Looking at the water is very soothing. In other words, just do your best to feel tranquil, detached and mentally neutral. Then, ask yourself the following questions and write down the answers:

A. What are your life dreams?
B. In what way have you realized your life dreams?
C. What would need to happen in your life for you to feel fulfilled and self-actualized?

D. What professional objectives excite you the most when you imagine yourself achieving them?

E. Who are your professional heroes and whose career do you admire or envy?

F. Where do you see yourself in 5, 10 and 20 years?

G. What do you sense is so important to you that you would regret not doing?

Being brutally honest with yourself may take you back to feeling stuck in the uncomfortable territory of impasse. It may open a can of fears and regrets....

Important: be kind and patient with yourself, become your own best friend. An impasse is not a failure. Instead, it's a necessary crisis, a call to shift your perspectives, to evolve, to move forward, to break free from fear.

5. Visualize –Experience Your Desire ('It'); Activate All Your Senses

In everyday life, you are rarely aware of *your ability to feel your vision*, to sense a full-bodied (emotional and physical) response to the images that you gather while being led through a guided meditation. Envisioning your dream career allows images as in a vivid dream to enter your subconscious mind.

Not only can you see, feel and smell your vision but, most amazingly, you can receive a signal from your intuition about who you are, what's unique about you, what is right for you.

In order to come to this clear space, first you need to silence the noise in your head. This involves separating your self from the mind chatter and barrage of fearful thoughts and opinions. You can find recordings of guided meditations and visualizations at **daretochangelife.com/ shop.html**

Visualization exercises bring to mind images of work, environment, and the types of activities and people that you would like to be surrounded by. These images tap into your awareness and your intuition in addition to activating all your five senses. They elicit your full-bodied vivid experience of the imagined situation and yourself in it in the present time, not in the future.

The feelings and body sensations that arise while visualizing yourself, or being led through the visualization, will reflect aspects of self-awareness that you may not be cognizant of yet.

They will give you a clue as to how you may feel and act if these circumstances were to come about for real in your life. Notice your body sensations: Do you feel excitement and joy or discomfort, pain and fear?

Once you finish the visualization, write down highlights from the exercise: the images, feelings and body sensations that arose for you while being in this imaginary world. If you were excited and filled with joy, you may want to explore this vision further because you have tapped into your subconscious and received the green light to move in the direction of your bliss!

6. Ask God for Guidance

It was a really tough time in my life; some call it a midlife crisis. I felt lost, stuck and a failure. All my prestigious degrees, experiences and achievements didn't help. I knew that I could not continue doing business as usual. I needed a change but was as much afraid of any changes as I was afraid of not changing. I know that feeling of impasse can be scary and perplexing.

Feeling really desperate, I turned to a Higher Intelligence – God – and asked for guidance. These were my prayers:

"Dear God, please help me find the clarity and conviction that my life matters. I am open to receiving your guidance."

"Dear God, please help me bring back my strength and find my path in this life…. Please guide me to a life of personal freedom, abundance and significant contributions."

"Dear God, please help me restore my faith and patience. I surrender myself to you completely…."

"Dear God, please guide me to a life where my gifts and talents will be used for a higher purpose… in the perfect space and time."

I invite you to use my prayers if they resonate with you. Be open to receive!

CHAPTER 4

You Know What You Want to Do, But How Do You Get There?

"The greatest glory in living lies not in never falling, but in rising every time we fall."

~ Ralph Waldo Emerson

While you are mining for your best career path, your focus needs to be on the *What* rather than the *How*. Once you get an idea of what you would like to do *to make a life* as opposed to *making a living*, you can move to the next phase and start thinking about *How* – what are the steps to get to what you want to do.

Important: Note that finding your dream job is not a precise science. You may fail a few times; you may lose your compass and confuse priorities. You may even feel alone and completely exhausted. If it happens, allow yourself to pause and regroup. Learn from your mistakes but don't despair. Persevere by the strength of your conviction and maintain focus on your vision.

From a big picture viewpoint, you will need to cultivate the following four pillars in order to succeed at your endeavors:

1. **Knowledge, Skills and Credentials**
2. **Confident Decisiveness, Self-Reliance and Action**
3. **Important Associations, Support and the Advice of Professionals**
4. **Marketing and Assertive Promoting of Your Services and Products**

Let's take a closer look at these pillars of success.

1. Knowledge, Skills and Credentials

If you don't yet have information about requirements for your new occupation, do your homework. Can you transfer your current skills and experience into your new career choice? If yes, great! If not, do not despair. Instead, find out which additional skills or credentials you need to acquire in order to achieve your professional goals.

Do you need to go back to school to study nutrition, psychology, marketing or finance? Will hiring a coach provide the support and assistance you need to achieve your goals? Does the work that you are aspiring to do require formal education and licensure or will self-study and experience suffice? Find out and get going!

Most occupations now require a variety of expertise but don't get yourself overwhelmed – you may choose to master them one at a time. If you feel that there is a gap in your knowledge-base that stands between you and your vision, get busy!

Public libraries could be a great place to start your research. You may also sign up for pertinent teleseminars or webinars and obtain a lot of valuable information that way. You can learn useful information, often free of charge, and also get the opportunity to connect with experts and test their systems at no risk or cost.

There are a lot of educational seminars, workshops and associations in almost any area of interest. There are internship and volunteering opportunities. Whether it's marketing, negotiation skills, media exposure or accounting, you can find ways to obtain the necessary knowledge to fill the gaps or hire professionals to assist you.

2. Confident Decisiveness, Self-Reliance and Action

If you are really sick and tired of feeling stuck and wasting your life while envying others' successes – get excited, get angry, get passionate and…ACT. Don't worry about other people's opinions about whether your career choice is good for you. You are in charge of your life and your decisions. Be willing to bear the consequences of your choices and get ready to stand up for what you know is right for you!

Confident decisiveness will help you deal with worries and the 'what if' paralysis; it will provide you with a sense of control and allow you to grow in self-confidence. This is the way to personal freedom!

When you exude confident decisiveness, people around you feel it and respond with respect and interest, sometimes even admiration. It works whether you are an employee, a consultant or a business owner. This quality inspires others and encourages cooperation and support. It comes from your inner conviction, from your resolve to live your life in a way that feels right for you!

Here is the caveat: if you want to be in control of your life as opposed to drifting through it unfulfilled and unhappy, you must be willing to take full responsibility for your emotions, decisions and actions. I love what Daniel S. Kennedy stated in his book *The Ultimate Success Secret:*

"You will continue to be unimportant as long as you depend on others to make you feel important."

"You will continue to be un-prosperous as long as you depend on others to make you prosperous."

"You will continue to be uninspired as long as you depend on others to make you inspired."

I would add that you will continue to be unhappy as long as you depend on others to make you happy.

Most likely, you will encounter a few challenges while implementing your career vision. But instead of focusing on the obstacles and complaining about the reasons you cannot get to your goal sooner, get creative and focus on the solutions and opportunities.

The real challenge is not the obstacles or the mistakes you make along the way, but your willingness to be self-reliant and take responsibility for your situation. The key is to act with confidence and with your eye on a possible solution, regardless of external circumstances.

The fear of making mistakes often immobilizes

people from taking actions. Then guilt, worry and anxiety take over and you lose your drive and confidence. The simple secret of avoiding this fear of mistakes trap is taking action by making even small steps toward your vision.

If you make a mistake, course-correct to incorporate the new understanding you now possess! Action, like daylight, evaporates the fear of 'what if' and empowers you.

Another ingredient of success is to *always celebrate your wins*, because *what you focus on expands!* When you focus on what works, on your achievements (regardless how small they may be), you give energy and power to your successes instead of your mistakes. You get on a 'success vibration' and your success grows!

I invite you now to practice making some adjustments to the words and phrases you use in your thinking and speaking that can dramatically affect results as you move from being confused to self-reliant:

Indecisive	Confident
I need to	I will
It's hard	I can do it
I don't know how	I'll figure it out
I don't have time	I'll make time for it
Complaining	Grateful
Fearful	Resourceful
Regretful	Optimistic

3. Important Associations, Support and the Advice of Professionals

The old adage, "It's not what you know but who you know that matters," often holds true in life. You may have doors open for you just by association with the 'right people' and pertinent organizations. This happens when you publish articles in relevant magazines, newspapers or blogs; join professional associations; and share photographs of yourself with well-known professionals in your field on your website. Establish accounts on LinkedIn, Facebook, Twitter and other social media outlets. Your membership in professional associations helps you build your credentials and create a professional network.

Surround yourself and spend time with positive, smart and inspiring people. You will need to take action to find these people but it's worth the effort. Don't squander your dreams by being lazy, stubborn or cheap.

Sometimes doing everything yourself is not the best strategy if you feel you can accomplish more by seeking the advice and assistance of coaches, lawyers or others professionals.

Obviously, the Internet has an enormous amount of useful information. Spend some time browsing in your subjects of interest. You may also find and talk to people in your field – professionals who do what you are inspired to do.

Find experts in your field of interest and establish a connection with them. Sign up for their program, invite them to lunch or schedule a virtual meeting or informational interview.

You may even get the opportunity to observe top experts in your field live and in person! Obtaining advice from those who succeeded in their profession and in the kind of work you're inspired to do is priceless.

If your current financial situation allows you to sign up for a specific seminar or program that you believe will provide the necessary skills and exposure to the right people, go ahead and invest in your career and yourself. I like to use shortcuts where appropriate, available and possible.

4. Marketing and Assertive Promoting of Your Services and Products

If you have an important message to convey, a service or product to offer, you must learn how to get exposure and promote them. In every professional field, every business or occupation, those who are good marketers and promoters, win.

It may not be comfortable or easy for you to promote yourself, your products and your services. Note that this false belief about being modest when it comes to self-promotion may be one of the biggest obstacles you face in your career.

Instead of criticizing those who are good at promoting their message and their offerings, learn how to become really good at this skill. Looking at others and comparing yourself to them will leave you envious and broke, both emotionally and financially. Instead, research all the possible ways that you can promote your service, product or message and get busy.

Waiting to be discovered and recognized, working hard and expecting to be noticed and promoted rarely works in real life. *C'est la vie.*

It's not enough to be the best at what you do – you must learn how to let the world know that you are valuable, that your services and products will solve people's problems and therefore, are important for them.

CHAPTER 5

Skilled Communication is Your Secret Weapon

"Communication is a skill that you can learn. It's like riding a bicycle or typing. If you're willing to work at it, you can rapidly improve the quality of every part of your life."

~ Brian Tracy

We use the word 'communication' often in professional and personal life and there is a very good reason for it. It is a tool, a lever and a 'secret weapon,' figuratively speaking. It allows you to come across as a true professional, to set boundaries and convey your message with clarity.

Good communication leads to having relationships that are based on respect and mutual benefit and to achieving your goals. It's a 'must have' skill for overall success in life.

You probably know that there are two types of communication: verbal and non-verbal. Both are equally important, so let's look at a few aspects of communication.

You Don't Have a Second Chance to Make a First Impression

When you have an interview (whether you are the interviewee or interviewer), or any other meeting for that matter, your body language is critical. Your confident posture, eye contact, firm handshake, friendly smile, respectful manners and positive attitude can make or break your chance of success.

Way too often there are smart, skilled people that lack awareness of their body language or their manners (non-verbal communication). The assumption that having skills, knowledge and even experience should be enough to land a good job or have a successful business rarely works.

The way you present yourself – whether it is through eloquent verbal self-expression, a confident handshake, direct eye contact or respectful demeanor – creates an immediate initial impression about you. And you can control these 'levers' if you are aware of them!

If you exude arrogance, superiority or disrespect for other people's opinions, beliefs or boundaries, you cut your chances of a good outcome and lasting relationship.

If you come across as 'high maintenance' due to your opinionated attitude or 'what will I get in return?' expectations, people will try to avoid your company no matter how much knowledge or experience you have. As the old adage says, "Nobody cares what you know until they know that you care."

On the other hand, when you are genuinely considerate and attentive to others, exude kindness, respect and confidence through your demeanor, words and actions – you attract people and earn respect effortlessly. Once you feel confident and come across as a considerate and respectful person, your energy becomes naturally more inviting and peaceful.

Make Effective Phone Calls

Have you ever received a phone call where the caller starts with, "Hi, I need to find out…" or "Hi, can you help me with…?"

I have, and my immediate reaction was "Why should I?" When a caller doesn't use words like 'please,' 'how are you today?' 'would you be able to…,' 'would you be so kind as to help/clarify/resolve…' – I feel disturbed. Do you?

Unfortunately, we don't get lessons on verbal and non-verbal communication at schools or colleges but it is so important! When you want a person on the other side of the phone line to help you resolve a problem, find information or clarify something for you, using words that convey respect for his/her assistance can motivate or the responder to assist you.

If you express your questions or request using a respectful intonation and polite words – most of the time, you will get adequate assistance and a reciprocal polite attitude. Realize that people can choose to be very helpful and attentive or unsupportive and indifferent. You can influence others' response by choosing your own attitude.

Acknowledging people for their willingness to assist you, recognizing their effort, time and good will leads to better connection, motivation and a more satisfying experience for both the giver and the receiver. Always recognize and acknowledge good work, great attitude and positive results.

Honest and heartfelt acknowledgement always makes a difference in communication, sometimes a profound one. Don't withhold your sincere praise for the assistance you receive due to fear of inappropriateness or for any other reasons. Find ways to express your appreciation and acknowledgment and be prepared for miracles!

Below are a few suggestions for making effective phone calls:

1. **Opening:** Always start the conversation with, "Hello, how are you today?" Then, introduce yourself and, if appropriate, ask the responder whether it's a good time for him/her to speak with you right now. This question is very important because it displays your respect for the other person's time and schedule. If you receive an OK to continue the conversation, then you may proceed. Otherwise, ask what time would be convenient for a call back.

2. **Express the reason for your phone call:** Be clear and concise while expressing your inquiry or posting

questions. You may choose (if pertinent) to confirm that the person on the other line understood you well by asking, "Do you follow me?" or "Have I explained the situation clearly?"

3. **Follow up:** if pertinent, ask if it's OK to follow up on your inquiry and ask when would be a good time for this person to receive another call from you.

4. **Closing:** Always finish your conversation with a sincere, heartfelt acknowledgement. Express appreciation for their help, assistance, time, attention, etc. (e.g. "I really appreciated your help today," or "Thank you so much for your assistance," or "I appreciate you taking time to talk with me."

Be aware of how you conduct your phone calls. Pause, take a few moments before calling to collect your thoughts, and practice your acknowledgement skills on people you don't know well or don't know at all. This skill alone makes the world a happier place.

Write Emails Like a Pro

From my numerous email exchanges, whether people write them to me for the first time or respond to my emails, I've noticed how small details and the intonations of emails make a difference in the way I interpret the message and experience its sender.

Below are my observations about writing emails and subsequent suggestions:

1. **Name:** When you use a person's name, it automatically makes the email more personal and less formal.

2. **Opening:** When you start your email with a focus on the other person (e.g. "I trust all is well," or "I hope all is well," or "How are you?" "How is your new job going?"), it comes across as you being considerate and polite.

3. **Call to Action:** Once you write the body of your email, whether it is a request for help, an inquiry or a 'catching up with you' kind of email, have a 'call to action' phrase that is pertinent and appropriate (e.g. "Look forward to hearing from you," or "Please advise," or "Please clarify what I am missing here.").

4. **Closing:** Always finish your email by expressing appreciation for something (e.g. "Thank you for your kind attention and assistance," or "I appreciate you taking time to meet with me," or "I truly appreciate all the help you offered.")

5. **Mirror the sender's communication style:** Each person has a preferred communication style. If you receive a brief text or email, be brief in your response as well (if possible). If the sender's email is formal and impersonal, respond in a respectful yet unemotional/ formal manner. If the person prefers text or email instead of a phone call, notice it and communicate with them 'in kind' – via email or text.

Gain awareness of the 'unspoken guidelines' of your written communication and notice how it affects the outcome.

Should You 'Be Yourself' at Work?

I would like to answer this question with my favorite 'it depends' answer. I am a big believer in setting and respecting boundaries, in both your personal and professional life. As Dr. Phil McGraw, a prominent psychologist and TV show host, often states, "You teach people how to treat you."

If 'being yourself' means sharing your personal or financial challenges with your colleagues at work, whining about not being satisfied with your job or complaining about particular co-workers or managers to your other colleagues – then NO, it's not a good idea to 'be yourself' at work! I believe that a true professional should not bring any personal issues to work. They should act responsibly and respectfully in the work environment.

Things come up in everybody's life – financial ruin, relationship challenges, personal losses and health issues. Many may disagree with me, but I feel that these matters must be handled outside of the work environment.

I realize that it's often not easy because most people build personal relationships in their workplace. But professionalism assumes being responsible for the environment you create around yourself, for knowing and respecting your own and other people boundaries.

One common mistake I have noticed some people make when they start a new job or a business is asking too many questions and often disturbing and distracting others' work. When you feel that you do not understand something, instead of asking questions, rely on yourself to find answers.

You will be better off researching the subject yourself first and really making a concerted effort to find a solution to the problem on your own. If you don't find a desired answer after that, then it's appropriate to ask questions. This way, you come across as self-reliant and resourceful individual.

You don't teach co-workers to treat you with respect by simply expecting or demanding it. You teach people to respect you by the way you conduct yourself at work. The way you speak and act, the way you handle personal and professional challenges, your attitude and work ethics all factor into the impression you create.

A personal drama that you may be going through right now in your home life has no room in your workplace. Any work conflicts should be resolved by conveying your values and boundaries calmly and clearly, with dignity and respect toward others.

If 'being yourself' means employing honesty in a diplomatic way, acting with confidence and in consideration of others, being aware of your own boundaries and respecting others' boundaries, then it's a good idea to 'be yourself' at work.

I recall working for a major financial institution with

a colleague who was well respected by his co-workers and managers. One day I learned that he had some personal misfortune and lived out of his car for a substantial length of time before he was able to regain his financial footing. Not once did he complain or share his personal drama at work! This guy was a pro at maintaining boundaries between his personal and professional life.

Dare
to Change
Life

You Are What You Think

"You see things and say, 'why?' but I dream
things that never were and say, 'why not?'"

~ George Bernard Shaw

Most people are unaware of how many limiting beliefs they hold in their subconscious mind and how these core beliefs sabotage their lives. These 'mental weeds' or unquestioned/unexamined limiting beliefs are formed over many years, especially during childhood. They require conscious awareness and commitment to be replaced by supportive and inspiring beliefs.

In the process of living, every person experiences challenging circumstances, disappointments, heartbreaks and despair. However, some people still manage to lead joyful and meaningful lives. Others, in the meantime, feel unlucky, bitter and discontent throughout their lives.

The major difference is the way you think about yourself, your possibilities and opportunities. Yes, your way of thinking is the most important factor that determines your success in life – personal and professional.

Life Happens to All

Have you ever had a time in your life when everything seemed to be falling apart, perhaps at the same time, despite your best efforts and intentions? Did you feel trapped, lost and hopeless? You are not alone.

Life happens to all of us. But what determines the quality of your life is what you choose to do when you realize that you chose the wrong career or made a bad investment or agreed to partner with the wrong person.

When you feel the need for a change – act! You must find the tools, strength and support to get yourself back into the 'driver's seat'. You must choose yourself in order to steer toward your deliberate destination, toward the grand vision for your life. The best place to start is with adjusting the way you think about yourself and your life.

Be Aware of Your Limiting Beliefs

The ways you respond to life's adversities are often rooted in your subconscious limiting beliefs about yourself. These limiting beliefs have a greater capacity to ruin your life than the adversities themselves.

The process of controlling your thinking is the most challenging and the most important discipline in your life. It involves establishing a personal life philosophy that reflects your values in life and positively influences your way of thinking, your decisions and actions.

Once you are able to purposefully choose how you want to *BE* – *how to perceive and respond to the events in your life* – instead of simply drifting with the winds of challenging circumstances, your experience of living will change dramatically both personally and professionally.

Only one question remains, and that is how to deal with your limiting beliefs. My suggestion is to eliminate them and replace them with supportive and empowering beliefs by tuning into the 'source energies' within you.

The stronger your awareness of the inherent and constant streams of wellbeing energies within you, the weaker your limiting beliefs will become. I invite you to follow these recommended daily practices to create a shift in your thinking:

Wake up time: Express what you are grateful for this morning. *Gratitude is a catalyst for positive thinking and the flow of abundance.* When you look at your reality with appreciation, you feel better about your life because you see the world through the eyes of God.

Bedtime: Count at least five 'wins' – achievements you had that day, regardless how big or small they were. Counting your 'wins' allows you to feel that you are making progress. 'Success begets success' and this simple daily discipline trains your mind to focus on successes rather than failures and disappointments.

Never Ever Give Up on Your Dreams

Over the years, you probably had a number of aspirations and dreams that you discounted as impossible, unrealistic or impractical. Whether your friends, family or societal 'norms' influenced your choices and decisions or your own insecurities and fears – somehow, you trained yourself to censor your creative visions.

I know that keeping your dreams alive at times does seem impossible. It takes clear intention and discipline to train yourself to believe in your vision even if it may seem unattainable for you right now. It always requires courage, perseverance and patience.

It may feel lonely when people around you are unsupportive. However, your aspirations are uniquely yours and you need to trust your inner wisdom. Mahatma Gandhi said it beautifully, "Don't listen to friends when the friend inside you says, 'Do this.'"

Develop a discipline to cancel fearful thoughts and instead focus on, give energy to exciting and inspiring thoughts. I suggest that you find a phrase that really works for you and reminds you to attend to and remove your 'mental weeds' promptly so they don't take over your thoughts.

For example, I like to challenge my fear of action by this simple question: *"Why not try?"* or with the statement, *"It doesn't have to be perfect – you can correct and improve. It's time to act."*

Finally, ask yourself: "What would I do if I absolutely positively believed that I am supported and would succeed no matter what?"

I love what Neale Donald Walsch wrote, "The mind is the last part of yourself to listen to. It thinks of everything you can *lose*. The heart thinks of everything you can *give*, and the soul thinks of everything you *are*."

It is imperative for you to get really clear about *who you are, what you want* and *what you are willing to do* to live your purpose, your vision. *Embrace your otherness, appreciate your uniqueness and take pleasure in being the best you can be.* Find your own path that reflects your goals and values and matches your talents and creative aspirations.

Carve your distinctive path to your vision. Strive to live your purpose, your best life and NEVER EVER GIVE UP! It's up to you who you want to BE and what life you want to create for yourself…. Shift from powerless longing to empowered manifestation!

About the Author

Millen Livis is a courage igniter and a possibilities catalyst. She works with women who want to get unstuck, who yearn for more vitality, abundance, freedom, joy, meaning and love in their lives.

An author, entrepreneur and a career and empowerment coach, Millen believes in the power of a healthy attitude, an inspiring vision and personal empowerment. The diversity of her personal experience makes her a firm believer that each of us has a unique path and purpose in life that is waiting to be discovered.

Through her coaching, books, guided meditation and relaxation recordings and live retreats, Millen helps women rediscover their authentic power and create lives of freedom, abundance and purpose.

Schedule a complimentary discovery session at **daretochangelife.com**.

Other books in the

Dare to Change Life series

A Shift toward Optimal Health:
Secrets To Holistic Healing

This book is a compilation of the author's personal experiences with different natural healing systems. It offers practical holistic approaches to restore and maintain your optimal health naturally.

A Shift toward Abundance:
Secrets To Financial Freedom

This book questions your relationship with money that is defined by your subconscious beliefs about abundance, scarcity, debt, the actual use of money in your life and financial responsibility. It offers practical ways to release drama around money and start living an abundant life.

A Shift toward Love:
Secrets to Harmonious Relationships

This book covers a wide spectrum of your relationships—from the relationship with yourself to your partner, your ex, children, parents, siblings and friends. It candidly discusses practical ways to reclaim your wholeness and transform your relationship with.others.

Thank you for reading my book–I hope you enjoyed it!

Your review of the book is VERY important – it helps me create valuable content for my readers and clients. I would really appreciate it if you could go to the retailer where you purchased the book and write your review. Additionally, if you would like to receive a review copy of my next book in the "Dare to Change Life" series, please feel free to contact me here: **millenlivis.com/contact-2/** or email me directly at **millen@daretochangelife.com**

~ Millen Livis

NOTES

NOTES

NOTES

NOTES

NOTES

Dare
to Change
Life

www.ingramcontent.com/pod-product-compliance
Lightning Source LLC
Chambersburg PA
CBHW071024040426

42443CB00007B/915